WORLDWIDE EVANGELIZATION
A STUDY IN ACTS 13–28

BIBLE STUDIES TO IMPACT THE LIVES OF ORDINARY PEOPLE

Written by Esma Cardinal

The Word Worldwide

CHRISTIAN FOCUS

For details of our titles visit us on our website
www.christianfocus.com

ISBN 1-84550-005-9

Copyright © WEC International

Published in 2004 by
Christian Focus Publications Ltd, Geanies House,
Fearn, Tain, Ross-shire, IV20 ITW, Scotland
and
WEC International, Bulstrode, Oxford Road,
Gerrards Cross, Bucks, SL9 8SZ

Cover design by Alister MacInnes

Printed and bound by Bell & Bain, Glasgow

All rights reserved. No part of this publication may be reproduced, stored in a retrieval system, or transmitted, in any form, by any means, electronic, mechanical, photocopying, recording or otherwise without the prior permission of the publisher or a licence permitting restricted copying. In the U.K. such licences are issued by the Copyright Licensing Agency, 90 Tottenham Court Road, London, WIP 9HE.

CONTENTS

PREFACE 4
INTRODUCTORY STUDY 5

QUESTIONS AND NOTES

STUDY 1 – PICKED FOR A SPECIAL JOB 8
STUDY 2 – UNCIRCUMCISED GENTILES ALSO? 12
STUDY 3 – A LOOK AT THREE HOUSEHOLDS 15
STUDY 4 – A TALE OF THREE CITIES 19
STUDY 5 – PRISCILLA'S STORY 23
STUDY 6 – WHATEVER NEXT! 26
STUDY 7 – MISSIONARY JOURNEYS SUMMARISED 30
STUDY 8 – WE WERE THERE 34
STUDY 9 – TWO YEARS IN CAESAREA 38
STUDY 10 – ARRIVAL AT LAST 42

ANSWER GUIDE

STUDY 1 48
STUDY 2 49
STUDY 3 50
STUDY 4 51
STUDY 5 52
STUDY 6 53
STUDY 7 54
STUDY 8 55
STUDY 9 56
STUDY 10 57

PREFACE
GEARED FOR GROWTH

> 'Where there's LIFE there's GROWTH:
> Where there's GROWTH there's LIFE.'

WHY GROW a study group?

Because as we study the Bible and share together we can

- learn to combat loneliness, depression, staleness, frustration, and other problems
- get to understand and love each other
- become responsive to the Holy Spirit's dealing and obedient to God's Word

and that's GROWTH.

How do you GROW a study group?

- Just start by asking a friend to join you and then aim at expanding your group.
- Study the set portions daily (they are brief and easy: no catches).
- Meet once a week to discuss what you find.
- Befriend others, both Christians and non-Christians, and work away together

see how it GROWS!

WHEN you GROW ...

This will happen at school, at home, at work, at play, in your youth group, your student fellowship, women's meetings, mid-week meetings, churches and communities,

you'll be REACHING THROUGH TEACHING

INTRODUCTORY STUDY

NEWS ... NEWS ... NEWS

What are your chief sources of information? Television? Internet? Print? Radio? Public speeches? Telephone? Private conversations? Any others?
Discuss in your group how you learned about a recent

Earthquake,
　Space exploration,
　　Medical breakthrough,
　　　Massacre,
　　　　Political upheaval.

Most news these days is: bad? frightening? good? entertaining? How do you react to stories most frequently broadcast?

Many people are saying they want more 'good' news. But what is good news? Has it gone so far out of fashion that a definition eludes us?

The New Testament is full of good news. In fact it is the stupendous, good news of Jesus Christ. The English word most often used for it is 'gospel'. We sometimes call it the 'evangel' from the Greek *euangelion*. So to spread the gospel, to proclaim the good news of salvation, is 'evangelization'.

God intends that the whole world will hear the gospel. Jesus Himself proclaimed it. 'Repent and believe the good news.' He preached in Mark 1:15. He said that 'the gospel must first be preached to all nations' (Mark 13:10) and that Christians would be witnesses 'to the ends of the earth' (Acts 1:8). He told the disciples to go into 'all the world and preach the good news to all creation' (Mark 16:15).

Every living person has the right to hear the gospel, otherwise how can they believe and be saved by the one of whom they have not heard? (Rom. 10:14). The second part of the book of Acts recounts the ever-widening areas in which the evangel was proclaimed and the church established. Following chapter 12 we are introduced to a different world in chapter 13. The church's centre moved from Jerusalem to Antioch. Peter had been the leading preacher; Saul (Paul) took his place. Focus for evangelization was soon broadcast from the Jewish nation to all nations as God had promised Abraham (Gen. 12:3).

THE FIRST-CENTURY WORLD
Three great civilizations had contributed to the world into which Christianity burst. They were the Greek, Roman, and Hebrew influences.

1. Greek
In 330 BC Alexander the Great spiralled to a pinnacle of power higher than any monarch had ever reached. The civilization he and his successors spread helped shape government, science, medicine and the arts, even to modern times. What did it mean for the evangelization of the known world in Paul's day? One benefit was the Greek language. Because it was readily understood, Paul and his party had no need to learn a foreign language, and no need for an interpreter. The Old Testament which had been translated into Greek (the Septuagint) was the Apostles' Bible.

2. Roman
After a time Rome displaced Greece as ruler of the Mediterranean world and was the dominant power during the New Testament period. Because of this civilization, barriers which had previously separated nations were down, providing a unified world for the gospel to penetrate. The peaceful conditions of the Pax Romana on land and sea enabled Christ's messengers to travel unhindered. Under Caesar Augustus ten thousand labourers built a network of long-lasting roads. Thus Christian missionaries travelled with a minimum of danger and delay along the roads used by Caesar's legions and merchants.

3. Hebrew
But it was the presence of Jewish men and women throughout the Roman Empire that provided the most fertile soil for sowing gospel seeds. The dispersions of 722 BC and 586 BC had scattered Judaists so widely that it was reported in the first century AD: 'It is hard to find a single place on the habitable earth that has not admitted this tribe of men, and is possessed by it.' With them went the worship of the one true God, the expectation of a coming Messiah, and the Septuagint Scriptures. Their synagogues became religious and cultural centres and even attracted many Gentile proselytes, as well as some known simply as 'God-fearers'. Though Paul was called an 'apostle to the Gentiles' his heart was with his own Jewish people. He always went first to the synagogue community who had at least some understanding of God's ancient promises. The evangel was not pumped into a vacuum.

Sick Human Race
Clearly the course of history had shaped circumstances to prepare the world for the good news of Christ's coming. In addition, the sad state of the human race cried out for a cure which only the Saviour could supply. Symptoms of society's sickness appear in the New Testament. Read quietly Acts 16:16; I Corinthians 5:9-11; 6:9-11; Galatians 5:19-21; Ephesians

2:1-3; 4:17-19; 5:3-8; Colossians 3:5-8; I Peter 2:18-20. Some of your group have probably read or seen films of corruption and cruelty in the Roman Empire. Add this information to what you found in the Bible verses above. Then in a few words describe the 'world' of that period (What's changed? you may ask!).

IMPACT OF THE EVANGEL
The good news of salvation reached the known world within a few decades. Much detail of its spread has been lost to history. Certainly Luke (writer of Acts) has not told the whole story; Paul's letters hint at a much wider proclamation. We do know that Christ changed countless lives in that period, and that groups of believers came together in widely separated places. There must have been scores of gospel bearers, apart from the few found in the New Testament.

TWO SUGGESTED PROJECTS
1. While working through this study book, follow the course of the story on maps which can be found in many Bibles. Where possible, ascertain modern names of countries and cities.
2. Try to discover what has taken place there since the end of Acts (c. AD 62). Perhaps each group member can choose one place of interest, e.g., Jerusalem, Malta. Does the New Testament give information on later events? Was a strong church established there? What has happened in the two thousand years since then? What about the modern situation? Is Christianity strong there now? Can you unearth something in particular to prompt you to pray for people there? Can you possibly help send the gospel to that spot on the earth? Or even go yourself? Apart from Bible commentaries, look for information in missionary literature, encyclopaedias and church history books. Make brief notes on your findings and share them with the group when 'your' city or country comes up in the studies.

THE BIG QUESTION
How completely has worldwide evangelization been accomplished?

STUDY 1

PICKED FOR A SPECIAL JOB

QUESTIONS

DAY 1 *Acts 11:25-30; 12:25-13:3. Syrian Antioch.*
a) Imagine that you are an outsider. You walk in to a meeting of the Antioch church. Describe your first impression?

b) Who was their 'Lord'? How important is He in the church?

DAY 2 *Acts 4:36; 9:15, 26, 27; 22:22-26, 30; 12:25; 13:1-4.*
a) Of the two men chosen to be sent out, what made the first-named a suitable companion for the other?

b) What is the compelling force behind the two missionaries on this journey?

DAY 3 *Acts 13:4-12. Cyprus.*
a) Compare Elymas the Jew with Sergius Paulus the Roman.

b) Did the Jew's religious background guarantee a right kind of faith?

c) The governor (proconsul) was astonished. Note carefully what it was that touched him deeply.

QUESTIONS (contd.)

DAY 4 *Acts 13:13-26. Pisidian Antioch.*
a) Do you detect a note of authority in Paul's introduction? (13:16).

b) What use did Paul make of the history of his race?

DAY 5 *Acts 13:23, 32-39, 48, 52. Pisidian Antioch.*
From these verses trace the stream of good news, and its effect. Discuss how the same gospel changes lives today.

DAY 6 *Acts 14:6-18. Lystra.*
a) The missionaries preach in a pagan area where God's power heals a man. In the surprising scene that follows, does it seem that the crowd understood Paul's message?

b) How did Paul and Barnabas feel about their new-found popularity?

DAY 7 *Acts 14:1-17, 19-22. Iconium, Lystra, Derbe, Antioch.*
a) What does Paul accept as an inevitable consequence of following Christ? (14:22). And look at 1 Thessalonians 3:4; 2 Corinthians 6:4-10.

b) In what ways are Christians badly treated today?

NOTES

'Set apart for me Barnabas and Saul for the work to which I have called them.'

Who heard the call?
Over the sixteen years since Jesus died, rose again and returned to the Father, groups of Christians had appeared in widely scattered cities. Antioch in Syria was one important centre. The believers had matured through the teaching of prophets and the teachers who knew the secret of successful church life: giving Jesus Christ the central place. They worshipped, served, ministered to the Lord, and fasted. It was to these church leaders that the Holy Spirit spoke about a special task waiting for two of their number.

Who was chosen for the special work?
The first-named, Barnabas, was already known with affection among Christians. He was generous, faithful, Spirit-filled, an encourager, a teacher, a good man in every respect. The other, Saul, had frightened the church years earlier. But that was before he met the risen Jesus Christ on the road to Damascus. In more recent times Saul had teamed up with Barnabas, and together they helped establish the Christian group in Antioch. A man of Jewish education and Roman citizenship, Saul knew from the day of his conversion that he was to play a vital part in God's kingdom.

Getting ready for the work
Some of the travel was to be by ship, and some over land. Try to imagine what preparations needed to be done. The Bible leaves us guessing about unimportant detail, and tells us the facts that really matter. We read nothing about packing food, medicine, clothes, etc., and of challenging valedictory meetings. All we know about preparations and goodbyes for this first missionary journey is contained in one short verse: 'So after they had fasted and prayed, they placed their hands on them and sent them off' (13:3).

The special job. What was it?
In a nutshell: to go cross-culturally and spread the great news of salvation through Jesus. On their first trip the two missionaries went straight to Barnabas' home, Cyprus, working their way across the island before heading for several strategic mainland cities. Their approach was single-minded for, as they pointed out in Pisidian Antioch, they carried responsibility to 'bring salvation to the ends of the earth' (13:47). Some hearers were hostile, others receptive, while still others carried their enthusiasm too far, mistaking the two men for gods. Through it all, they made Jesus known as Messiah (Christ) for the Jews, and the way to salvation for all people.

The need is the same today
From that day to this, people everywhere have needed, and still need, to know that 'God so loved the world that He gave His one and only Son, that whoever believes in Him shall not perish but have eternal life' (John 3:16). The special job for some Christians is overseas, cross-cultural evangelism. Church leaders attuned to the Holy Spirit will be aware of His instruction to set apart this one and that one for the work to which He has called them. The chosen ones will always be the right people whom God has prepared. He picks appropriate workers for particular work. Once called, obedient Christians do what needs to be done in preparation. And very importantly, their home churches identify with them in prayer, and send them off.

STUDY 2
UNCIRCUMCISED GENTILES ALSO?

QUESTIONS

DAY 1 *Acts 14:23-28.*
a) Consider why the whole church in Antioch would be keen to hear a report from Paul and Barnabas.

b) From today's reading can you see two sides to the door of salvation?

DAY 2 *Acts 15:1-5; Ephesians 2:8, 9.*
a) Certain Jewish Christians (including Pharisees) said that Gentiles must be .... and obey the .... in order to be Christians.

b) A Pharisee himself, Paul opposed such teaching. Why?

DAY 3 *Acts 15:6-11; Matthew 5:8.*
a) Peter reminded the church of what happened ten years earlier (Acts 10). What do you see as central to his speech in Acts 15:7-11.

b) Discuss the practical outcome of a 'pure heart' (15:9; Matt.5:8).

DAY 4 *Acts 14:27; 15:3, 4, 12.*
a) According to Paul and Barnabas, who was responsible for the success of their first missionary journey?

QUESTIONS (contd.)

b) Neither success nor outward legalism caused Paul to boast. See Galatians 6:14 for the basis of his glory.

DAY 5 *Acts 15:13-21; Amos 9:11, 12.*
Adding to Peter's recounting of earlier acceptance of Gentiles, Paul and Barnabas relate to the whole Jerusalem church the wonderful things God has done for the Gentiles during their travels. James sums up the discussion, quoting an Old Testament prophet, Amos. Do you know other places in the Old Testament which promise salvation for all races, not only for Jews?

DAY 6 *Acts 15:19-29.*
What four practices, common in the pagan world, were to be avoided?

DAY 7 *Acts 12:12, 25; 13:13; 15:30-41; Colossians 4:10; 2 Timothy 4:11.*
From the scattered references to John Mark in these verses, we can piece together a picture of his family life, possibly a lack of stickability, and in the end his worth as Paul's helper. Can we find encouragement here?

NOTES

Two thousand years on, no eyebrow is raised at the news of Gentiles becoming Christians. Many of us are non-Jews. We have always known that Gentiles too can be a part of God's family. Why, then, did their salvation grow into such a huge problem in AD 48?

It had never occurred to the Jews who formed the first church that the gospel message could be applied to those outside the Jewish race. So the conversion of Gentiles in Caesarea took them by surprise (Acts 10 and 11). Then when idolaters in central Asia Minor and in Antioch accepted Jesus as their Saviour it raised a hard question for the home church. Some said just trusting the Lord was not enough. Unless those people were circumcised and kept Moses' law they could not be saved. The missionaries disagreed. They said, 'People are not saved by believing in Jesus and something *else*. Salvation is by faith.'

To understand the Judaisers' viewpoint we need to remember the importance of the law, especially circumcision, to the Jews. God had given them the law as a covenant to last forever. Some Jewish Christians had not yet understood how completely Jesus Christ's coming had fulfilled all the requirements of that law. It was not surprising therefore that they wanted to cling to Jewish tradition. They saw keeping the commandments as part of coming into the Christian church. In order to maintain oneness between all Christians, Jewish and Gentile, everyone must be a Jew.

The dispute became so sharp that the matter was referred to the apostles and elders in Jerusalem. After a long debate it was Peter, Barnabas and Paul, the three who had seen evidence of God at work in Gentile lives, who presented the crux of the matter. Their argument went like this: God clearly called us to preach the Lord Jesus Christ to Gentiles; he is doing wonderful things for them; the Holy Spirit lives in them; we Jews are not able to keep the law perfectly; we are all saved by Christ's grace; why make it hard for the Gentiles?

It remained for James, the church leader, to agree with the missionaries and to suggest regulations against certain practices to which many Gentiles were prone, and which disgusted Jews. Acceptance of these requirements broke down both religious and social barriers. The principle was established that Jews and Gentile were one through Jesus Christ, not through law-keeping.

For a clearer picture of these matters read the letter to the Galatians. Some Bible scholars believe Paul wrote it in about AD 48, before the Jerusalem Council, to the churches established on his first journey.

In the light of Acts 15:11; Galatians 2:16 and Ephesians 2:8,9, consider these extra questions:

- To what extent should we expect other Christians to follow the same religious customs as we do?
- Is my lifestyle controlled by local culture? Scriptural teaching? A mixture of both? Anything else?
- Should missionaries expect new converts to become westernised? Why, or why not?

STUDY 3
A LOOK AT THREE HOUSEHOLDS

QUESTIONS

Paul and Barnabas had parted company. Silas had joined Paul on his second journey.

DAY 1 *Acts 16:1-5; 2 Timothy 1:1, 2, 5; 3:15.*
a) The young man taking John Mark's place comes from a mixed marriage. He seems well-suited to the task. What do you see as Timothy's main qualification?

b) How would you fit into this category?

DAY 2 *Acts 16:6-8.*
a) The Holy Spirit prevented them from preaching in .... and ....

b) When our plans are thwarted, how do many of us act? What did Paul and his party do?

DAY 3 *Acts 16:9, 10.*
a) What specific guidance came to Paul, and how did he respond?

b) Should Christians today be ready for similar immediate action?

QUESTIONS (contd.)

DAY 4 *Acts 16:9-15.*
Trace the circumstances which contributed to bring Lydia to faith in Christ.

DAY 5 *Acts 16:16-21.*
a) Why was Paul troubled about the slave girl's actions? How accurate were the words she shouted?

b) When the girl was set free from the spirit, the men who had been exploiting her were hostile because of their:
  1. love for their slave,
  2. loyalty to the Roman government,
  3. concern for peace in the community,
  4. greed for money,
  5. dislike of the Jews.

Discuss your preferred answer/s with your group.

DAY 6 *Acts 16:22-34.*
In verse 25 we see how Paul and Silas followed what Jesus taught in Matthew 5:11, 12. What evidence do we find that the gaoler is saved?

DAY 7 *Acts 16:35-40.*
The authorities change their minds; Paul and Silas are released; a group of Christians meet in Lydia's home. How did these changes come about?

NOTES

A Lystran family
The people of Lystra in Galatia (modern-day Turkey) told an old legend about Zeus and Hermes (Jupiter and Mercury) and were afraid of not recognizing the deities if they should appear as men. Perhaps that is why Paul and Barnabas, with their extraordinary power, were mistaken for the gods. Since the town had been made a Roman colony about fifty years earlier it became the home of military men who enjoyed the privileges of Roman citizenship.

One household in Lystra comes into prominence, where a Greek is married to a Jewess. The wife is a Christian, as is her mother, and her son, Timothy. Just when Paul first met Timothy is not clear. Perhaps the young man witnessed the lynching recorded in Acts 14:19. See what Paul wrote to him in 2 Timothy 3:10,11. What a blessing for a young man to have a grandmother and mother who follow the Lord and pass on His teaching to the children! We wonder how the Christian mother and grandmother, and the non-Christian father, felt about Timothy's decision to go off on missionary work. Do you know of similar family situations in our day?

Lydia's household in Philippi
As it turned out, Paul's next major move, to the West and not the East, became a crucial turning point in history. Philippi, the group's first stop, was a leading city in Macedonia in the north of Greece. It had a proud history, bearing the name of its founder Philip II, the father of Alexander the Great. The Egnatian Way (main highway to Rome from the East) ran through Philippi, and ruins of its culture and prosperity have been found. The large number of retired Roman military personnel there had little time for the Jews which could be the reason that few Jews had settled there and no Jewish synagogue had been established.

Outside the city walls, by the River Gangites, a group of women met for prayer on the Sabbath. Lydia, a Gentile, believed in the Jews' God. Why, how and where her conversion took place we are not told, but probably it was in her home town of Thyatira where a number of Jews lived. This well-to-do lady had come to Philippi on business and apparently rented a sizeable house for her household and for commerce. With a love for the true God as a background Lydia gladly allowed the Lord to open her heart to the good news Paul shared with them. This successful business woman and all who lived with her were brought to Christ; she offered hospitality to the evangelistic team; she was not ashamed of Paul and Silas after their imprisonment; a church was born in her home. Is such a scenario likely today?

The Philippian Gaoler's household
God did something special for another Philippian home, quite different from Lydia's. Head of this house was a Roman civil servant, the local gaoler. During the hours of one ordinary night some extraordinary events turned the prison guard and his whole family upside down. Or right side up! Duties that night included securing a couple of battered and bleeding 'trouble-makers' in the stocks of a dark, damp, reeking underground cell. When a violent earthquake shook the gaol and freed the prisoners the terrified officer had only one thought: suicide. But suddenly he was snatched from the brink of a lost eternity, his life and his soul saved. In a Christ-like gesture he took Paul and Silas home for a meal and treated their wounds, which he had probably inflicted himself. His influence extended to his household for they, too, believed in the Lord and were baptised. No wonder the whole family was filled with joy (v. 34). From the verge of suicide to the start of a new life in Christ! Are miracles like this still possible?

STUDY 4
A TALE OF THREE CITIES

QUESTIONS

DAY 1 *Acts 17:1-4. Thessalonica.*
From these verses discuss Paul's method of evangelism. Do you know someone who might respond to the same method and message?

DAY 2 *Acts 17:5-9. Thessalonica.*
a) Verse 5 begins with 'But' and leads into an entirely different picture. What prompted the opposition?

b) Does the basis of their resentment seem legitimate?

DAY 3 *Acts 17:10-15. Berea.*
a) Luke makes an observation about Bereans and Thessalonians in verse 11. What big difference was there between the Jews of the two cities?

b) When we hear a new line of teaching, what reliable guide can we consult?

DAY 4 *Acts 17:16-23. Athens.*
Make a list of religions and philosophies in Athens. Can Athenians of that period be described in one word?

QUESTIONS (contd.)

DAY 5 *Acts 17:24-31. Athens.*
What impresses you about God, as presented in these verses?

DAY 6 *Acts 17:3, 18, 32-34. Athens.*
Paul often talked and wrote about resurrection. Why is it central to New Testament teaching? See also Romans 1:1-4; 6:8-11 (Notice carefully that resurrection is neither reincarnation or transmigration).

DAY 7 a) Think of yourself as a Thessalonian, or a Berean, or an Athenian. Would you join in a demonstration against Paul in Thessalonica?

b) Would you gladly follow the Lord in all three places?

c) Would you put off making a decision until another time, as some did in Athens?

NOTES

THESSALONICA, today's Salonica in northern Greece, was a busy seaport 160 kilometres from Philippi. Its main street formed part of the Egnatian Way. As capital of Macedonia with 20,000 population, its location made it important for trade and communication.

17:2	Paul's learning and preaching ability earned him acceptance for three consecutive weeks at the synagogue. He probably spent more than three weeks in the city.
17:4	A large number of Gentiles attached to the synagogue joined Paul, as well as women of high rank. But only a few Jews believed.
17:5	Non-responsive Jews grew jealous over proselytes accepting Jesus as Messiah. It seems Paul and Silas had stayed in Jason's home.
17:6, 7	A mixture of truth and lies in the charge made it difficult to refute. The accusation of political insurrection was a gross exaggeration.
17:9	Jason and friends had to guarantee no further disturbance.

BEREA, about 80 kilometres from Jerusalem.

17:11	Berean Jews are praised for their open-minded attitude. They studied their Scriptures (our Old Testament) every day to see if Paul's startling new teaching was right.
17:12	Honest Bible study led many to faith in Jesus Christ.
17:13	There is no evidence that opposition began with Bereans.

ATHENS was the capital of the great Grecian empire which had brought education and art and love of physical culture to the known world. But in Paul's time the glory had gone from Athens, which was now under Roman power. There were no great artists nor sculptors. In the old Athens there had been something mighty of which to be proud; but today the people were idle, careless and without the gifts which had raised them in the past. A visitor could see the marvellous statues to the gods and goddesses and athletes, the exquisite buildings and temples. It was said that it was easier to meet a god than a man in Athens. Athenians loved going about in the market and asking one another, 'What's new?'

17:15, 16	We can imagine Paul sightseeing while waiting for his friends. If he found employment in the city he would be observant, trudging to and from work.
17:18	Epicurus (4th century BC) taught that the pursuit of pleasure is man's chief business. To Stoics everything that happened must be accepted without resentment. Some saw Paul as just one more 'babbler' who paraded scraps of knowledge he had picked up, without giving it much thought. Because

	of confusion over the word for resurrection, they thought he spoke of a certain goddess.
17:19	Areopagus, or Mars Hill, or Hill of Ares, was the place of Athens' supreme court where Socrates was condemned to die. The court's main interest in Paul's day lay in new religious ideas and gods. Paul did not face a formal trial here.
17:22	He saw them very religious in all respects, too religious, very reverent, deity-minded, as superstitious as possible (depending on the translation we read). Was this a compliment, or a rebuke? Or a vague, tactful remark?
17:23	They erected altars to unknown gods for fear of omitting any deity.
17:28	Paul referred to Stoic poets, Aratus and Cleanthes. His literary education was useful.
17:29	Perhaps he pointed to man-made idols of gold, silver and stone as he spoke.
17:31, 32	To speak of the dead being raised was like dropping a bomb on these Greeks.

Look again at verse 16. Neither the city's cultural history nor the beauty of its present art moved Paul. It was the permeating idolatry of society that upset him for he knew that 'the sacrifices of pagans are offered to demons' (I Cor. 10:20). Think how different his discussions would have been had he been an average sightseer! His speech at Athens (vv. 22-31) is significant as an approach to those idolatrous pagans.

Paul needed to establish contact with his prestigious audience who had no background in Jewish teaching, and did so by acknowledging their religious nature. He went on to claim first-hand knowledge of the God they yearned for. This God is the maker of all things, Lord of everything, and far above living in man-made shrines. As judge, He expects people to turn from their evil ways, and has proved it all by raising 'a man' from death! According to the record, the interruption came before the name of Jesus was spoken. But by the time Paul left Athens a group had been converted. At least one, Dionysius, was a member of the council, of the intellectual aristocracy.

***

Following his usual habit Paul went first to the synagogue in all three places, to build on the Jews' understanding of God and His promises. Whereas in Athens matters were taken out of the Jews' hands (and Luke did not record their response), in both Thessalonica and Berea, Jews and God-fearing Greeks believed in Jesus. Read the first Thessalonian letter and sense the delight of Paul, Silas and Timothy. Next to his own relationship to the Lord, Paul's chief joy was always in the growing faith of others.

How about us? How keenly do we care about each other's spiritual growth?

STUDY 5
PRISCILLA'S STORY

QUESTIONS

DAY 1 *Acts 18:1-4, 18, 19; Romans 16:3, 4; 1 Corinthians 16:19.*
a) Describe Paul's weekly activities during his early days in Corinth?

b) Paul's friendship with Aquila and Priscilla was at first based on their trade as tentmakers (or leather workers). How did their relationship develop over the years?

DAY 2 *Acts 18:5-8.*
From these verses choose at least one important fact. You may want just to think about it, or tell it to someone, or put it into practice, or pray about it. An interesting group discussion will result as you pool your ideas and experiences.

DAY 3 *Acts 18:9-11.*
a) Why would Paul need such a reassuring message from the Lord?

b) In writing to Christians in Corinth later, he described how he felt when he was with them (1 Cor. 2:1-5, specially v. 3). What central truth dominated his ministry in Corinth?

DAY 4 *Acts 18:12-17.*
a) Have you, or anyone you know, ever been taken to court for talking about Jesus?

QUESTIONS (contd.)

b) Notice how the Lord's promise to Paul in verse 10 came true through Gallio.

DAY 5 *Acts 18:18-23.*
a) Much activity condensed into a few sentences! Follow Paul's travels on a map. What seems to be Paul's main aim as he goes from place to place?

b) Can today's Christians follow his example when they travel?

DAY 6 *Acts 18:24-28.*
Was Apollos' education in Alexandria a useful preparation for preaching and teaching? Read verse 24 in several versions.

DAY 7 a) Make a list of every person in chapter 18. How much are we told about each one? (Nationality, position, attitude to Christ, etc.). What part did they play in the spread of the Gospel?

b) What will you try to copy, or avoid?

NOTES

I have always had a soft spot in my heart for Corinth. It was there that Aquila and I first met our good friend Paul, and it was during our stay in Corinth that the church was born. In fact, we were part of that first small group. We all grew in our Christian faith, especially through Paul's teaching.

My husband and I had to leave Italy when the Emperor Claudius expelled all Jews from Rome, following confusion and riots. While our friends went in all directions, we decided to settle in Corinth for a time, and work at our trade. Looking back, I feel sure the move was part of God's plan.

We found Corinth to be a big city, busy with commerce. It also had a reputation for loose living. The Lord Jesus had changed all our lives and we loved to discuss the many ways He has fulfilled the Scriptures.

Sabbath was the highlight of the week as we went to the synagogue to worship God and hear His Word being read. Once Paul started going with us, I noticed a difference in the topics of discussion. As a teacher, he was often invited to speak, and took every opportunity to try and convince everyone that Jesus is our Messiah.

Then when Silas and Timothy arrived with cheerful news of the Macedonian converts (and I think they brought a gift of money for Paul) he seemed gripped by a new surge of passion for the evangel. From then on he gave his whole time to preaching. Unfortunately some of the Jews grew more and more bitter, and concocted evil stories about him. I well remember the day when things came to a head. Paul was so outraged that he shook out his clothes and told them in no uncertain terms that he would leave them alone now. He would concentrate on the Gentiles from then on.

Paul got involved with an amazing variety of characters during his eighteen months in Corinth: Gentile God-fearers, a Roman governor and countless others. Some joined us as Christians, some were antagonistic, many remained indifferent.

Apollos was another friend who greatly helped the Corinthian church. My husband and I admired him immensely when we first heard him speak of Jesus at the Ephesus synagogue. But we could see gaps in his understanding. Recognizing the enormous possibilities in this brilliant orator, we invited him home and pointed out more correctly the way of the Lord. Any nervousness we may have felt soon disappeared. Highly educated Alexandrian though he was, Apollos listened respectfully as if we were his parents, and thanked us for our help. Everyone knows now of the impact he made on Corinth. The pity is that divisions came, with some claiming Paul, and some Apollos, as leader. The Holy Spirit surely gave Paul wisdom in dealing with this squabble in his letter. Some of my favourite reading is in chapters one to three of First Corinthians. I hope it will be re-read for centuries to come.

(*Editor's note*: It is!)

STUDY 6
WHATEVER NEXT!

QUESTIONS

DAY 1 *Acts 19:1-7; Mark 1:4-8.*
a) What did Paul discover about Ephesus?

b) The group were ignorant of an essential part of John the Baptist's teaching. How did Paul add to their understanding?

DAY 2 *Acts 19:8-10.*
a) What strong views were expressed?

b) If these people of Asia are lost eternally, who is to blame? Why?

DAY 3 *Acts 19:11, 12.*
a) What sort of miracles took place? Who performed them?

b) Which word of verse 11 suggests that the miracles were not common? See also Acts 5:12-16.

DAY 4 *Acts 19:13-17; 3:1-8, 15, 16.*
a) Does the use of the Lord Jesus' name always work wonders?

QUESTIONS (contd.)

b) Why did Sceva's sons not have the same success as Peter in Acts 3? From Acts 19:13-17 can we see that something good resulted?

DAY 5 *Acts 19:18-22.*
a) If new Christians today had a bonfire like this one, what would they burn?

b) How would the news media report the event?

DAY 6 *Acts 19:23-31.*
a) Demetrius was anxious about two outcomes of Paul's preaching (vv. 25-27). What were they?

b) 'Missionaries should be careful not to threaten local customs.' Do you agree or disagree with this advice?

DAY 7 *Acts 19:32–20:1.*
a) Make notes on the main points of the town clerk's speech in verses 35-40. Assuming the silversmith and the town clerk spoke truthfully about Paul, how can we reconcile verse 26 with verse 37?

b) As an extra, you may like to write an account of the book-burning and riot in Ephesus, and how it all ended, for a newspaper or radio or TV news item.

NOTES

Seven years after setting out on his first missionary journey, Paul came to Ephesus. Every drama you could imagine had crossed his path: beatings, tiresome travelling, imprisonment, constant preaching, mistaken identity, successful evangelism and church growth. Surely this new venture would produce nothing new! If this is what he thought, he was wrong. Chapter 19 records a few incidents from two years in the city, each more amazing than the last.

'Disciples' of incomplete Christianity

The ministry of John the Baptist as a forerunner of the Lord Jesus Christ had finished a generation earlier. John himself knew that he merely pointed to the one still to come (Matt. 3:11). How strange that a John the Baptist movement should continue alongside the Christian movement! His preaching always contained warning of condemnation, therefore 'Repent!' he thundered. Paul saw that what the group needed, was simply the Saviour Jesus. It was a case of 'No Holy Spirit, no Jesus. No Jesus, no Holy Spirit'.

Lows and highs

Opposition to Paul's preaching in the synagogue became almost commonplace. But his heart ached every time the Jews rejected his message. As always, the numbers of believers in the Lord grew as he found new places for spreading the word. An exceptional wave of evangelism is confined to the few lines of verse 10.

Extraordinary miracles, outrageous mimicry

The superstitious Ephesians thought that healings came through Paul's working clothes. These were probably sweat bands worn on his head, and aprons for the waist. The truth was, of course, that the power came from God as Paul prayed in the name of Jesus.

The exciting news of miraculous healings prompted some Jewish charlatans to try and imitate Paul, with disastrous results. In a city abounding in sorcerers and magicians the outcome taught a much-needed lesson: the name of Jesus must not be used as magic.

Public bonfire

Books of any kind were valuable in those days, but none so rare and precious as those containing formulas of magic and incantation. Yet those who saw the error of their ways were ready to abandon the evil inherent in their practice of the occult. Whether these were believers not previously willing to make a clean cut, or new believers, we do not know. In any case they proved their renunciation of all evil by publicly burning their scrolls. An enormous sum went up in smoke in an act of true repentance. What exciting times for Paul the preacher!

What a riot!
Paul's heightened reputation and the wonderful conversion of large numbers led to the next tumultuous episode in Ephesus. As a background do a little research on Ephesus, Diana (Artemis) and the temple. You will find a Bible Handbook useful here.

The main demonstration against 'The Way' and in favour of 'Artemis of the Ephesians' is typical of mob hysteria which still erupts today. It was all so confusing that Luke wrote (perhaps with a chuckle) that 'most of the people did not even know why they were there' (v. 32). Look at his descriptive words: a great disturbance, this fellow Paul, furious, uproar, rushed as one man, confusion, shouted for two hours. Then came the quiet influence of the city clerk who put an illogical case for stopping the commotion.

How did Paul react to the day's tumult? We can imagine him and his friends breathing a sigh of relief as the crowds dispersed, and thanking God for protection.

But what next? Does Paul decide enough is enough? Will he now look for an easier, less complicated way to serve the Lord?

STUDY 7

MISSIONARY JOURNEYS SUMMARISED

QUESTIONS

DAY 1 *Acts 20:6-12.*
a) What two kinds of food did the people share on that first day of the week at Troas?

b) Do you know why the teenage boy went to sleep?

DAY 2 *Acts 20:17-21; 19:4, 5; Ephesians 2:8.*
Discuss the central point of what Paul taught the people of Ephesus.

DAY 3 *Acts 20:25-35.*
a) In Paul's colourful language, who are the sheep, shepherds and wolves?

b) Where will 'wolves' come from? Does the danger still continue?

DAY 4 *Acts 20:36-38; Ephesians 3:14-19.*
a) Try to imagine what Paul prayed for at their parting. The prayer in his letter to the same church about three years later was mainly for: Their health? Business success? Spiritual growth? Increase in numbers?

b) How should we pray for each other?

QUESTIONS (contd.)

DAY 5 *Acts 21:1-6.*
The words 'we' and 'us' suggest that Luke, the writer of Acts, was part of the action. In today's verses how does Luke indicate that he saw and heard what happened?

DAY 6 *Acts 19:21; 20:16, 22-24; 21:4, 10-17.*
What do you think of Paul's determination to reach Jerusalem?

DAY 7 From this week's readings in Acts 20 and 21, choose one way Christians showed love for each other. Tell your group how you would like to see this carried out in the modern world. See John 13:35.

NOTES

No. Paul did not look for safer ways to scatter the good news.

More travel ... more farewells ... at least one more plot against him ... more warnings of danger ... all come to light in chapters 20 and 21. Soon after arriving in Jerusalem this time, Paul became a prisoner of the Roman government and remained so until the end of the Acts record. His 'Three Missionary Journeys' as they are called, had spanned eleven years, ending in about AD 57. At this point let's look as his chief activities as a travelling missionary.

Preaching

Some people laugh at the tale of Paul, the 'long-winded preacher' at Troas, talking all night until daylight next morning. But apart from one sleepy boy, the congregation seemed happy enough with the overnight meeting. Wouldn't we like to know all he said?

He probably followed the same guidelines at Troas as at Ephesus. There, he said, 'I have not hesitated to preach anything that would be helpful to you' (20:20), 'I have declared ... they must turn to God in repentance and have faith in our Lord Jesus' (v. 21), 'I have gone about preaching the kingdom' (v. 25), 'I ... proclaim to you the whole will of God' (v. 27), 'I never stopped warning you' (v. 31). His visit was the 'task of testifying to the gospel of God's grace' (v. 24).

Thank God for preachers of the same themes nowadays. May their numbers increase!

Praying

Preaching without praying is like trying to swim without water. In a mysterious way our Father God hears prayer in the name of Jesus, and acts in response. Paul's letters reveal the depth of his concern for people – a concern that drove him to prayer.

He remembered the Christians in Rome in prayer 'at all times' (Rom. 1:9, 10). For all Israelites he prayed 'that they may be saved' (Rom. 10:1). For the Christians at Ephesus Paul thanked God and prayed for wisdom, revelation and enlightenment (Eph. 1:15ff). He was thankful for the Philippian church, and always prayed for them (Phil. 1:3, 4). His continual prayer for the Colossians was that God would fill them with the knowledge of His will so that their lives would please the Lord (Col. 1:9, 10). That 'the name of our Lord Jesus may be glorified' was his prayer for Thessalonica (2 Thess. 1:11, 12).

Recognising his own dependence on the Lord, Paul begged his Christian friends to pray also for him. Modern missionaries, too, often request the same prayer backing: 'Pray also for me, that whenever I open my mouth, words may be given me so that I will fearlessly make known the mystery of the gospel' (Eph. 6:19).

Working with a team
While Paul took the lead on his preaching and teaching tours, he valued the help of his companions. For some examples of his appreciation see Romans 16:3, 4, 9 and Philippians 2:25; 4:3. The apostle put into practice what he taught about the body of Christ with every part playing a necessary role. The imperative for team work has not diminished over the centuries.

Spending time with people
Travelling by land and sea, preaching, teaching and praying ... Did these activities use up all Paul's time? No!

Don't forget that he worked for his living, at least some of the time. His hands supplied his own needs and the needs of his associates, and more than that, remembering the Lord's words: 'It is more blessed to give than to receive' he also worked to help the weak (20:34, 35). At one time he actually worked with other Christians (Aquila and Priscilla) thus spending time in their company.

In Troas Paul not only preached all night but 'broke bread' with all believers. Whether or not this was a supper in remembrance of the Lord, they made it an occasion for a fellowship meal.

Paul loved to visit people in their homes, going from 'house to house' (20:20). Wherever the team went, Christians offered hospitality. We can imagine the talking and laughter (tears too?) of the host families and their guests.

Fellowship in Christ will include listening, praying, reading, music, conversation, food and anything else that promotes the health of spirit, body and soul.

STUDY 8
WE WERE THERE

QUESTIONS

DAY 1 *Acts 21:17-26.*
Recall some of the incidents Paul could report to the Jerusalem church elders (21:19).

DAY 2 *Acts 21:27–22:2; 14:11-13; John 12:12, 13.*
a) Compare the moods of the three crowds in today's readings.

b) Do you agree with the idea that the mob is usually right?

DAY 3 *Acts 22:3-21.*
What impresses you most about Paul's speech on the castle stairs?

DAY 4 *Acts 22:21-29; 2 Corinthians 11:23-27; Philippians 1:29.*
a) The Roman centurion and the commander (chief captain) became alarmed when they heard that Paul ....

b) Can Christians always expect to be exempted from suffering?

DAY 5 *Acts 22:30–23:10.*
Explain a basic difference between Pharisees and Sadducees.

QUESTIONS (contd.)

DAY 6 *Acts 23:11; 19:21; Matthew 28:19, 20; Romans 1:9-15.*
a) How necessary was it for Paul to go to Rome?

b) Following the stressful events of the previous two days, what would the Lord's assurance mean to Paul? (23:11).

DAY 7 *Acts 23:12-35.*
a) More than forty non-Christian Jews vowed not to ....

b) Rewrite in a couple of sentences how Paul ended up imprisoned in Caesarea.

NOTES

James (Jerusalem Church Leader, brother of Jesus)
Another sleepless night ... how far am I responsible for Paul's latest troubles? You see, the elders and I were thrilled to hear what God had done among the Gentiles through him. But as Jewish Christians we couldn't ignore the rumour that he was telling Jews to give up our Jewish customs. So we persuaded him to get involved in a vow in the temple. This course of action would calm the current uneasiness, or so we thought. On the contrary it caused big trouble. Some Christians are saying Paul's action was wrong. Others believe he showed Christ-like grace in becoming like a Jew to win the Jews. They say his willingness to compromise a little was for the sake of the gospel. Who is right?

A Jew from Asia
At last! That troublemaker, Paul, will soon be quiet – forever I hope. I'm a loyal follower of Jewish customs and I'm angry at the way this man speaks against our law. All over Asia too! Before God we Jews simply *must* stop this blasphemy. Here in Jerusalem we've spotted Paul several times – still up to his old tricks. To top it all we saw him with Trophimus, a Gentile from Ephesus. What shocking behaviour! Everyone knows the strict law against Gentiles going into the inner court. Well, we stirred up the crowds against Paul and the last I saw of him the soldiers were carrying him into the barracks. It's a pity the mob didn't lynch him, but the Roman commander will fix him. Good riddance, I say.
...I've been thinking ...we didn't actually see Paul take Trophimus into the temple ... they were just walking down the street ... and I never really *heard* him say anything against our law ... he just keeps insisting that Jesus rose from the dead and is our Messiah ... Could we be wrong after all?

Claudius Lysias (Roman Commandant, Chief Captain)
A quiet moment, and time for a self-assessment of the last couple of days. During great Jewish feasts the atmosphere often becomes tense. My masters in Rome insist on civil order, and I dare not allow a riot. So we garrison the Fortress of Antonia with a cohort of a thousand men at feast time. When I heard about the uproar in the city I took some troops and ran down to see. The rioters were beating the man I now know as Paul. I had to arrest him for his own good. At first I thought he was the Egyptian leader of the Sicarii band – those rebels who hide daggers in their clothes and mix with the crowds. Three years ago they caused a great stir and threatened to capture the city. I thought the Egyptian had come back. I was surprised to hear this Jew speak in Greek and Aramaic. My next shock was hearing that Paul was born a Roman citizen. It cost *me* a lot of money for that privilege. And I had ordered him to be scourged! Later when I asked the Jewish Council to specify

Paul's misdeeds, not even they could settle on a reason for the commotion. I was nonplussed. Then when Paul's nephew told me my prisoner was to be murdered I had no option but to send him to Governor Felix at Caesarea. He is under tight security and I can only hope he arrives safely. I must say that this unusual little Jew has impressed me deeply.

STUDY 9

TWO YEARS IN CAESAREA

QUESTIONS

DAY 1 Acts 24:1-21; Matthew 5:11, 12.
How closely did Paul's experience (24:5-9) match Jesus' words in the Sermon on the Mount?

DAY 2 Acts 24:14,15; 1 Corinthians 15:12-19.
Who will rise from the dead? Is anyone omitted?

DAY 3 Acts 24:22-27.
a) How much did Governor Felix know about Jesus Christ?

b) Describe his response to the gospel. How typical is he of many people?

DAY 4 Acts 23:1; 24:16; 25:8.
a) How do these statements of Paul fit in with his confession in 1 Timothy 1:15, 16?

b) Acts 22:25-29; 25:10-12 (Optional question). Does standing on his rights as a Roman citizen fulfil God's plan for Paul? Refer to the first question for Study 8, DAY 6.

QUESTIONS (contd.)

DAY 5 *Acts 25:13-27.*
Governor Festus represents Roman justice in the province. Is the system seen in a good light in this episode?

DAY 6 *Acts 26:1-18; Colossians 1:12-14.*
a) How did Paul describe two opposite kingdoms, and who are the rulers over them?

b) In which kingdom do we find forgiveness of sins?

DAY 7 *Acts 26:19-32.*
Describe the moods of Festus and Agrippa in verses 24-32.

NOTES

Three Officials
It is about AD 57 and Paul is a prisoner of the Roman government in Caesarea, capital of Judea. From here he will set out on his last recorded journey – to Rome, Gentile capital of the world. Before he leaves he stands before three representatives of officialdom: Felix, Festus and Agrippa.

Because Judea was considered a revolutionary province, the Caesar (emperor) governed it himself, as head of the army. He appointed a procurator (governor) to manage the region and to be accountable to him. In about AD 52 Emperor Claudius appointed Antonius Felix who had been first a slave, then a freedman, and who then climbed to high positions. Tacitus wrote that Felix 'held the power of a tyrant with the disposition of a slave'. After seven years he was recalled to Rome on account of his cruelty and misgovernment.

His successor was Porcius Festus, a more just and honest man than Felix. Festus died after two years.

Agrippa II was the last of the Herods. He ruled as king over a province north of Palestine. Drusilla, Bernice and Agrippa II were all children of Herod Agrippa I and although they were half-Jews they held strong pro-Roman views. Agrippa II lived initially with Bernice, causing a great scandal. When the couple made a formal visit to the newly-arrived governor, it was natural for Festus to consult Agrippa about the enigmatic prisoner in his charge.

Charge against Paul
The accusations brought by the Jews against Paul were eloquently presented by Tertullus acting as a prosecuting attorney. The first charge was political: Paul was a troublemaker, stirring up riots everywhere (24:5). If proven, this accusation would make Paul an insurrectionist liable to severe punishment. Tertullus knew that, while the Romans were tolerant of religion, they would never allow civil disorder.

Charge number two was sectarian: Paul was a ringleader of the Nazarene sect (24:5). Rome had already been troubled with false messianic movement that led to hysterical risings and bloodshed. The accuser knew the authorities could not disregard such a charge.

The third charge, of desecrating the temple, was most dangerous (24:6). The priests were Sadducees who collaborated with Rome, so to defile the temple was to infringe the rights of the pro-Romans. Tertullus hoped to incriminate Paul for this alleged crime of sacrilege.

In Defence of himself – and the Gospel
In response to the charges Paul maintained his claim to innocence. Ironically the temple visit referred to was in connection with gifts for the poor, and offerings (24:17,18). He was

ceremonially clean at the time. No official, from Claudius Lysias to Herod Agrippa, could find a reason for his death or imprisonment.

Paul's defence speeches carried more than self-justification; they included as much as possible about Jesus Christ. And so did his personal discussions with Felix and Drusilla. Some of his themes were:

> Faith in Jesus Christ (24:24).
> Judgment (24:25).
> Turning to God (26:18).
> Forgiveness (26:18).
> Longing for hearers to be saved (26:29).
> Resurrection. Even some Jews believed in this (24:15; 26:8, 23).

Personal response of officials
Felix and his Jewish wife were well-informed about 'The Way' (Christian teaching and activities) and were prepared to listen further. But on hearing the deeper matters of 'righteousness, self-control and the judgment to come' Felix grew frightened (24:25). And no wonder, for his past life fell far short of the high moral demands of God. Felix knew he ought to acquit Paul. For two reasons he left this innocent man under guard: he hoped for a bribe, and wanted to curry favour with the Jews.

Festus became famous in Bible history for his outburst to Paul in 26:28. Variously translated his words can mean, for example: 'Do you think that in such a short time you can persuade me to be a Christian?' (NIV) or 'You are with a little effort convincing enough to make me a Christian' (Berkeley). Whatever the translation, Agrippa's tragedy remains the same. He was so near and yet so far from the kingdom of God.

EXTRA QUESTION FOR DISCUSSION
How do we feel when we seem to fail as Paul did in his witness before Felix, Festus and Agrippa?

STUDY 10
ARRIVAL AT LAST

QUESTIONS

DAY 1 *Acts 27:1, 2; 20-26. At sea.*
a) How did Paul describe his close relationship to God in verses 23, 25?

b) Should we pray that faith in God will make us courageous?

DAY 2 *Acts 27:27-41. At sea.*
a) How did Paul set an example in verse 35?

b) Does the Lord care about mankind's need for food? Look at Matthew 6:9-11; 14:16-21; Romans 12:20.

DAY 3 *Acts 27:42–28:10. Malta.*
a) Find examples of kind actions and practical helpfulness on the island.

b) Do you notice something unexpected here?

DAY 4 *Acts 28:11-16. Malta to Rome.*
a) Name the three places where Paul and his friends met groups of Christian believers.

QUESTIONS (contd.)

b) Paul thanked God, and was encouraged (v. 15). In your present circumstances can you thank God for some recent event, and feel encouraged about the future?

DAY 5 *Acts 28:17-22. At Rome.*
a) Paul usually went to the synagogue on arrival in a city. Why did he ask the Jewish leaders to visit him this time?

b) Look at Philippians 1:12-14, 29, 30 and 2 Timothy 2:8-10. In the light of Paul's attitude to his chain, discuss the plight of Christians in prison today?

DAY 6 *Acts 28:23-29;* Isaiah 6:9, 10. *Rome.*
a) Paul told the Jews in Rome that some of them resembled their forefathers in Isaiah's day. What had they in common?

b) Think about this: 'There is no-one so blind as the one who doesn't want to see'.

DAY 7 *Acts 1:1; 28:30, 31.*
a) From the first to the last verse in this book, who is the central figure?

b) Luke seems to end the story abruptly. If you could meet him now, what would you like to ask him? Would you like to thank him for anything?

NOTES

At sea
Julius, an officer of the Emperor's Regiment, took charge of Paul and other prisoners for the journey from Caesarea to Rome. His kindness and consideration must have lifted Paul's spirits. Another encouragement was the devotion of Aristarchus who probably enrolled as Paul's slave in order to remain with him. Luke, too, was on board, perhaps as a servant.

In the middle of a raging storm, with no navigational aid and no prospect of escaping death at sea, everyone gave up hope. Then amazingly, a prisoner took charge. Paul alone found courage.

Still at sea
After two weeks of storm the sailors were relieved to hear the sound of breakers. They were approaching land. In the darkness the crew tried to escape in the dinghy but Paul again took the lead, frustrating their plan to desert the ship. In the early morning Paul (once more assuming control) made a sensible suggestion. He knew that all their physical powers would be needed in the next few hours. They must have something to eat.

Malta
Soon after their remarkable escape from the sea a snake fastened itself to Paul's hand. The islanders expected a bad reaction from the viper, suggesting that they knew it to be poisonous. To their superstitious minds Paul must be a murderer. Having escaped drowning, he was being pursued by 'Justice' for retribution. When they saw the snake did no harm, they quickly changed their minds. He was not a murderer after all, but a god! Popular opinion often swings from one extreme to another with little or no solid ground.

Malta to Rome
Seafarers of those times took seriously the images of their gods on the ship's bow and stern. The ship from Malta carried the Heavenly Twins, Castor and Pollux. Belief in their guardianship may have prompted the captain to leave in winter. To Syracuse (Archimedes' city) … to Rhegium (formerly a resplendent Greek city) … to Puteoli ('Sulphur Springs' on the Bay of Naples). Beautiful Mount Vesuvius could be seen from here. No-one knew that an awesome explosion would occur nineteen years later. At last Paul set foot in Italy.

Rome
The presence of Christians in Italy shows the widespread dispersion of faith in Christ by AD 60. Jews from Rome were visiting Jerusalem when the Holy Spirit came (Acts 2:5-11). Probably others also came with the Christian evangel over the years. Paul had written to

this church a couple of years earlier, saying how much he longed to see them. Not that he expected to come as a prisoner! The Roman church was mostly made up of Gentiles, with a good number of Jews as well. Their faith was already reported 'all over the world' (Rom. 1:8). They were soon to suffer under the notorious Emperor Nero.

For at least two years (possibly longer) Paul was under guard, waiting for trial before the emperor. Some snippets of information on his life in Rome are seen in these extracts from his prison letters.

Colossians	1:1-3; 4:7-14, 18
Ephesians	6:21, 22
Philemon	1:23, 24
2 Timothy	4:11-13

And then
Some believe that Paul made another journey after his release from imprisonment, and carried out his intention to take the gospel to Spain.

In heaven. Something to look forward to.
'After this I looked and there before me was a great multitude that no-one could count, from every nation, tribe, people and language, standing before the throne and in front of the Lamb. They were wearing white robes and were holding palm branches in their hands. And they cried out in a loud voice: "Salvation belongs to our God, who sits on the throne, and to the Lamb"' (Rev. 7:9, 10).

ANSWER GUIDE

The following pages contain an Answer Guide. It is recommended that answers to the questions be attempted before turning to this guide. It is only a guide and the answers given should not be treated as exhaustive.

GUIDE TO INTRODUCTORY STUDY

Although this study on Acts 13–28 may be used as a separate course, it will be helpful if the group members have first been through Acts 1–12. This one deals with many truths along the way, with the underlying theme of reaching the whole world with the gospel. Since Paul figures largely in this part of Acts, the studies could almost be called Paul's Missionary Journeys. We have tried to look beyond Paul to the great purposes of God Himself.

In this first week emphasize the meanings of 'gospel', 'evangel', 'evangelization', etc. Help the group to picture conditions in the then known world, and how well-prepared it was for Christ's coming.

Encourage individuals to take an interest in specific places or races (as suggested at the end of this first study). If there is time, begin to discuss recent missionary advances into some of these areas. Representatives of WEC International and other missions will be pleased to supply information. This will show that the Acts story is not an isolated period in history, but the coming of the church's growth which will continue till Christ comes.

Look ahead to Study 2, Day 6, where the New Age Movement is mentioned. Before reaching that week perhaps you, as leader, can do a little reading on the subject. It is not meant to take up too much time that week, but is important enough for some information to be shared as a warning.

GUIDE TO STUDY 1

DAY 1   a) There were large numbers; they were called 'Christians'; they gave generously; there were at least five leaders; they worshipped and fasted; they were sensitive to the Holy Spirit's directions, and ready to obey; they prayed.
b) Jesus was their Lord. He should always be the centre and focus of worship and ministry.

DAY 2   a) Barnabas was an encourager, showed discernment in bringing Saul (Paul) in as a teacher, good, full of the Holy Spirit and faith. He was already a co-worker with Saul (Paul).
b) Paul's earlier commission from the Lord. The Holy Spirit sent them.

DAY 3   a) Elymas would be expected to be interested in God's Word, but opposed to it. The Roman could oppose God's messenger, but wanted to hear God's Word.
b) Religious background does not guarantee anything.
c) The teaching about the Lord impressed the proconsul as much as (perhaps more than) Elymas' experience (v. 12).

DAY 4   a) He responds immediately to the invitation to speak. He says 'Listen to me!' as if he had the right to be heard.
b) He used it to show God's ancient plan is fulfilled in Jesus.

DAY 5   Jesus is the One who saves; He was raised from the dead; He forgives, justifies and gives eternal life. Those who believed were joyful, filled with the Holy Spirit (Encourage a clear understanding of the Christian gospel).

DAY 6   a) No. They thought the two men were gods.
b) Paul and Barnabas were appalled at the idea of being worshipped.

DAY 7   a) Hardships (tribulation, troubles). He endured subtle persecutions in some places, both physical and verbal, as well as outright violence.
b) There may be recent events in the news, near or far, or perhaps personal experiences.

GUIDE TO STUDY 2

DAY 1 a) These were the people who had sent Paul and Barnabas out about two years earlier. They would have been praying for the missionaries in their absence.
b) The people put their trust in the Lord (v. 23). God opened the door (v. 27).

DAY 2 a) … must be circumcised and obey the law of Moses.
b) Salvation is by faith in Christ. He has fulfilled the law.

DAY 3 a) Various themes: God has accepted Gentiles; he proved it by giving the Holy Spirit; it was by faith; their hearts were purified; both Gentile and Jew are saved by the grace of the Lord Jesus.
b) A 'pure heart' is more than a healthy organ pumping blood through the body! It signifies clean motivation for all of life, resulting in a good life.

DAY 4 a) God.
b) Christ and His cross, although crucifixion was shameful.

DAY 5 Genesis 12:1-3; Isaiah 49:6, and many others.

DAY 6 Food sacrificed to idols; blood (or bloodshed); meat of strangled animals; sexual immorality.

DAY 7 We do not know the reason for Mark's return to Jerusalem in Acts 13:13, nor do we know whether he can be blamed for the disagreement between Paul and Barnabas. However, he obviously proved his worth later. We can all take heart, no matter what our weak points have been.

GUIDE TO STUDY 3

DAY 1 a) He was a 'disciple', a 'believer'. He had a good reputation among other Christians. He had 'sincere faith' and knew the Scriptures.
b) Personal.

DAY 2 a) The province of Asia, and Bithynia.
b) Sometimes feel frustrated, push hard to get our own way. Some evaluate the situation and pray again for guidance. They took the road that was open.

DAY 3 a) The vision (v. 9) was taken as God's call to take the gospel.
b) Yes, when sure it is God's guidance.

DAY 4 She had come to Philippi from Thyatira. She already worshipped God. She met with others for prayer. Paul and his party came to Philippi in response to God's call. They went looking for those who met for prayer, and told them the gospel. The Lord opened her heart and mind to the message.

DAY 5 a) He recognized the presence of an evil spirit.
b) The words she shouted in verse 17 were true.
Greed was the main issue (v. 19), but they appealed to other issues which they hoped would sway the authorities.

DAY 6 They rejoiced when persecuted and accused falsely.
He showed kindness by tending their wounds and giving hospitality. He was baptised, and was filled with joy.

DAY 7 Many factors led to the good conclusion to Paul's visit to Philippi: he carefully followed the Holy Spirit's leading; he preached salvation in Jesus Christ; the power of the Lord got rid of an evil spirit; in their bad situation Paul and Silas had a positive testimony, etc.

GUIDE TO STUDY 4

DAY 1 He followed his custom of going to the synagogue on Sabbath days, and explained from the Old Testament how Jesus fulfils the prophecies. Some Jews believed, also some God-fearing Greeks and influential women. Some of the group may know Jesus.

DAY 2 a) Jealousy.
b) It was no basis for opposition.

DAY 3 a) The Bereans were prepared to give the message a fair hearing by examining the Scriptures every day to see if what Paul said was right.
b) We have the complete Bible as our guide.

DAY 4 Worship of idols (various religions). Jews and others who worshipped the true God. Philosophies: Stoic and Epicurean.
Paul described them as 'religious' ('superstitious').

DAY 5 Creator, sustainer, self-sufficient, sovereign, just, etc.

DAY 6 Much could be said about the resurrection of the dead. For example, Jesus spoke about His own resurrection (Mark 9:31); He did rise again (Mark 16); He also spoke about resurrection in the future (John 5:25-29). In I Corinthians 15 Paul argues that a risen, living Saviour is necessary for the gospel of salvation from sin, and for eternal life.

DAY 7 All answers are personal.

GUIDE TO STUDY 5

DAY 1 a) Worked at his trade with Aquila and Priscilla. On Sabbath (seventh day) went to synagogue meetings where he held discussions with Jews and non-Jews trying to convince them about Jesus.
b) They travelled together to Ephesus. Were fellow workers. Priscilla and Aquila took risks for Paul's sake, though we do not know what risks. Paul regarded them as close friends, and perhaps visited their house church.

DAY 2 Various possibilities, e.g., dedication to preaching, concern for Jews, whole household believes, baptism.

DAY 3 a) Opposition of Jews; perhaps he was tempted to give up; he felt weak.
b) The crucified Jesus Christ was his main theme.

DAY 4 a) This is more likely in some parts of the world than others.
b) The Roman official, Gallio, would not allow Jewish religious arguments to cause harm to anyone.

DAY 5 a) Corinth, Cenchrea, Ephesus, Caesarea, Jerusalem, Syrian Antioch, region of Galatia and Phrygia. To know and do God's will. To encourage Christians. To spread the Gospel.
b) God's will should always be our guide. Many opportunities can be found for witness and fellowship.

DAY 6 Yes. He had been trained to think and debate, and to understand Old Testament Scriptures. He knew a lot about Jesus.

DAY 7 Try to include each one, including Roman officials. A review of the chapter shows God using all kinds of people, in various ways, contributing to evangelization.

GUIDE TO STUDY 6

DAY 1 a) A group of twelve disciples following a 'John the Baptist Movement'. They knew about John's baptism as a sign of repentance, but did not know that John was only a forerunner of Jesus.
b) Paul explained what John had said about this, and about the Holy Spirit whom Jesus promised.

DAY 2 a) Paul was bold in his arguments; some hearers stubbornly refused to believe, they were outspoken in saying evil about 'The Way' (that is, faith in Jesus Christ).
b) They are responsible themselves because they were told the way of salvation.

DAY 3 a) Sick people were healed, and some spirits left some. God did the work of healing.
b) The word 'special' or 'unusual' or 'extraordinary' (according to the translation being used) indicates that the miracles had not been continuous.

DAY 4 a) No. It was not, and is not, to be used as magic.
b) Because they had no true faith in the Lord Jesus, they simply tried to imitate Paul. The event turned out for good as the Lord's name was given greater honour.

DAY 5 a) Anything that distracts from healthy, holy living. For example, drugs, ouija boards, tarot cards, crystals, pornography.
b) Some would report it as the activity of 'religious cranks' especially if believers made open confession as in verse 18.

DAY 6 a) Loss of trade (finance), and loss of honour for the goddess (religion).
b) All gospel preachers need wisdom in order to be true to the living God, while avoiding unnecessary offence (v. 37).

DAY 7 a) The fame of Ephesus and the temple of Artemis (Diana); Paul's innocence; legal means of dealing with complaints. Paul taught positive truth about the true God, but did not negatively act against their goddess.
b) Personal.

GUIDE TO STUDY 7

DAY 1 a) Food for the body (fellowship meal), and spiritual food (Paul's teaching).
b) We cannot know for sure but since Luke (a physician) mentioned the lamps and perhaps felt the heavy atmosphere himself, we assume they induced sleepiness. Besides, it was late, and the boy probably had worked all day.

DAY 2 The only way to know God is by repentance and faith in the Lord Jesus Christ. Luke records that Paul taught this when in Ephesus, and that he repeated it to the elders when they came to Miletus. And Paul wrote it in his letter to the Ephesians.

DAY 3 a) *Sheep*: Christians, people who make up the church.
Shepherds: Elders, or bishops, or overseers, or pastors, those responsible for the church.
Wolves: Teachers of wrong doctrines who sometimes use half-truths in order to confuse and deceive.
b) They emerge from both outside and inside (vv. 29, 30). The danger is always present.

DAY 4 a) We are not told, but can imagine it was similar to his recorded prayers. The prayer in Ephesians 3 was for all aspects of spiritual growth, including faith, love, power, etc. We can use Bible prayers as a model.
b) Personal.

DAY 5 The precise places visited, where the ships were headed, time spent with people, the beach farewell, all sound like a personal record. Authenticity like this adds to the historical authority of the book.

DAY 6 Some scholars think Paul stubbornly went against the Holy Spirit's leading. Others believe he was in the right. He obeyed God's leading, while aware of possible dangers. As it turned out, he got to Rome as a result.

DAY 7 Everybody's delight at Eutychus' recovery. Christians' sadness at parting. Hospitality. Paul's love for them seen in preaching, praying faithfully. Opportunities for showing love are endless.

GUIDE TO STUDY 8

DAY 1   Beginnings of church in Philippi; Gentiles coming to Christ in various places; etc.

DAY 2   a) *Jerusalem*, Acts 21: the Jews stir up trouble, the mob is confused and want to kill Paul.
Iconium, Acts 14: the heathen crowd want to treat Paul and Barnabas as gods.
Jerusalem, John 12: the Jewish crowd recognize Jesus as king of Israel.
b) A mob is easily swayed and often led by evil powers. But can be right sometimes.

DAY 3   Different people will be impressed by different things, e.g., Paul's sincerity, honesty, dedication, the abruptness of his conversion, the Lord's clear purposes for his life, etc.

DAY 4   a) Paul was a Roman citizen.
b) Suffering is to be expected, though it is not beyond God's power to prevent it.

DAY 5   Their opposing views on angels, spirits and resurrection (23:8). An easy way to remember: The Sadducees didn't believe in the resurrection, so they were sad.

DAY 6   a) Although the good news had already reached Rome and many other places, Paul wanted to go there to teach further. His desire was to play his part in the evangelization of the whole world. God had given him this task, and had promised an arrival there.
b) A great comfort.

DAY 7   a) Not to eat or drink anything until they killed Paul (If they kept their vow, there must have been forty dead Jews before long!).
b) Can be written in own words.

GUIDE TO STUDY 9

DAY 1 He was persecuted and falsely accused because of Jesus.

DAY 2 All, the righteous and the wicked.
No.

DAY 3 a) He was well-acquainted with the 'Way' (v. 22), apparently because of his years in the area. Then he let Paul talk to him often, partly in hope of a bribe.
b) He was unwilling to repent and believe at the time, putting it off for another day. Many people do the same thing, and never come to Christ.

DAY 4 a) He had always tried to please God, both before and after conversion to Christ. He realized that this was not enough, and learned to thank God for His mercy.
b) Paul reached Rome, but as a prisoner.

DAY 5 Yes, in the sense that a person had the right to a trial where he could defend himself. Also, a Roman citizen could appeal to the highest court in the Roman Empire.

DAY 6 a) Kingdoms of light and darkness, with God and Satan as rulers.
b) In God's kingdom, because of the death of Jesus Christ.

DAY 7 Festus interrupted Paul and shouted at him. Perhaps he felt guilty. Agrippa seemed to be thinking of his own need, while still unwilling to be a Christian. He was fair in his appraisal of Paul.

GUIDE TO STUDY 10

DAY 1   a) he belonged to God. He had faith in God.
b) Yes. Faith brings us into line with God's purposes, and we can be sure He will work according to His plan.

DAY 2   a) He ate some food, and thanked God.
b) Yes. He taught us to pray for it. He fed the people. We are to feed our enemies if they are hungry.

DAY 3   a) The islanders took pity on the 276 shipwrecked people, who would be wet, cold and tired. They lit a fire, probably under shelter of some kind. Paul helped gather sticks for the fire – no doubt others did too.
The island chief gave hospitality for three days. Paul showed concern for the chief's father: visited, prayed, and healed. Paul helped others who were sick. The islanders looked after them, and gave supplies when they left after three months.
b) Something unexpected? Although the centurion and Dr Luke were there, a prisoner (Paul) is presented as the main character in the story. Perhaps Luke helped in giving medical attention – but we do not overlook the power of God.
Notice that nothing is said about preaching on Malta.

DAY 4   a) Puteoli the Forum of Appius, the Three Taverns.
b) Personal.

DAY 5   a) He was chained to a guard, not allowed to go out into the city.
b) Paul accepted the situation and used it to make Christ known. This is not to say we ought not to work and pray for the release of people imprisoned unjustly.

DAY 6   a) They did not want to hear or see the truth.
b) Personal.

DAY 7   a) The Lord Jesus Christ.
b) Personal.

NOTES

OLD TESTAMENT

Triumphs Over Failures: A Study in Judges ISBN 1-85792-888-1 (above left)
Messenger of Love: A Study in Malachi ISBN 1-85792-885-7 (above right)
The Beginning of Everything: A Study in Genesis 1-11 ISBN 0-90806-728-3
Hypocrisy in Religion: A Study in Amos ISBN 0-90806-706-2
Unshakeable Confidence: A Study in Habakkuk & Joel ISBN 0-90806-751-8
A Saviour is Promised: A Study in Isaiah 1 - 39 ISBN 0-90806-755-0
The Throne and Temple: A Study in 1 & 2 Chronicles ISBN 1-85792-910-1
Our Magnificent God: A Study in Isaiah 40 - 66 ISBN 1-85792-909-8
The Cost of Obedience: A Study in Jeremiah ISBN 0-90806-761-5
Focus on Faith: A Study of 10 Old Testament Characters ISBN 1-85792-890-3
Faith, Courage and Perserverance: A Study in Ezra ISBN 1-85792-949-7
Amazing Love: A Study in Hosea ISBN 1-84550-004-0

NEW TESTAMENT

The World's Only Hope: A Study in Luke ISBN 1-85792-886-5 (above left)
Walking in Love: A Study in John's Epistles ISBN 1-85792-891-1 (above right)
Faith that Works: A Study in James ISBN 0-90806-701-1
Made Completely New: A Study in Colossians & Philemon ISBN 0-90806-721-6
Jesus-Christ, Who is He? A Study in John's Gospel ISBN 0-90806-716-X
Entering by Faith: A Study in Hebrews ISBN 1-85792-914-4
Heavenly Living: A Study in Ephesians ISBN 1-85792-911-X
The Early Church: A Study in Acts 1-12 ISBN 0-90806-736-4
Get Ready: A Study in 1 & 2 Thessalonians ISBN 1-85792-948-9
Worldwide Evangelization: A Study of Acts 13-28 ISBN 1-84550-005-9
Glimpses of the King: A Study of Matthew's Gospel ISBN 1-84550-007-5

CHARACTER

Abraham: A Study of Genesis 12-25 ISBN 1-85792-887-3 (above left)
Serving the Lord: A Study of Joshua ISBN 1-85792-889-X (above right)
Achieving the Impossible: A Study of Nehemiah ISBN 0-90806-707-0
God plans for Good: A Study of Joseph ISBN 0-90806-700-3
A Man After God's Own Heart: A Study of David ISBN 0-90806-746-1
Grace & Grit: A Study of Ruth & Esther ISBN 1-85792-908-X
Men of Courage: A Study of Elijah & Elisha ISBN 1-85792-913-6
Meek but Mighty: A Study of Moses ISBN 1-85792-951-9
Highly Esteemed: A Study of Daniel ISBN 1-84550-006-7

THEMES

God's Heart, My Heart: World Mission ISBN 1-85792-892-X (above left)
Freedom: You Can Find it! ISBN 0-90806-702-X (above right)
Freely Forgiven: A Study in Redemption ISBN 0-90806-720-8
The Problems of Life! Is there an Answer? ISBN 1-85792-907-1
Understanding the Way of Salvation ISBN 0-90082-880-3
Saints in Service: 12 Bible Characters ISBN 1-85792-912-8
Finding Christ in the Old Testament: Pre-existence and Prophecy
ISBN 0-90806-739-9

THE WORD WORLDWIDE

We first heard of WORD WORLDWIDE over twenty years ago when Marie Dinnen, its founder, shared excitedly about the wonderful way ministry to one needy woman had exploded to touch many lives. It was great to see the Word of God being made central in the lives of thousands of men and women, then to witness the life-changing results of them applying the Word to their circumstances. Over the years the vision for WORD WORLDWIDE has not dimmed in the hearts of those who are involved in this ministry. God is still at work through His Word and in today's self-seeking society, the Word is even more relevant to those who desire true meaning and purpose in life. WORD WORLDWIDE is a ministry of WEC International, an interdenominational missionary society, whose sole purpose is to see Christ known, loved and worshipped by all, particularly those who have yet to hear of His wonderful name. This ministry is a vital part of our work and we warmly recommend the WORD WORLDWIDE 'Geared for Growth' Bible studies to you. We know that as you study His Word you will be enriched in your personal walk with Christ. It is our hope that as you are blessed through these studies, you will find opportunities to help others discover a personal relationship with Jesus. As a mission we would encourage you to work with us to make Christ known to the ends of the earth.

Stewart and Jean Moulds – British Directors, **WEC International**.

A full list of over 50 'Geared for Growth' studies can be obtained from:

John and Ann Edwards
5 Louvaine Terrace, Hetton-le-Hole, Tyne & Wear, DH5 9PP
Tel. 0191 5262803 Email: rhysjohn.edwards@virgin.net

Anne Jenkins
2 Windermere Road, Carnforth, Lancs., LA5 9AR
Tel. 01524 734797 Email: anne@jenkins.abelgratis.com

UK Website: www.gearedforgrowth.co.uk

Christian Focus Publications
publishes books for all ages

Our mission statement –

STAYING FAITHFUL

In dependence upon God we seek to help make His infallible word, the Bible, relevant. Our aim is to ensure that the Lord Jesus Christ is presented as the only hope to obtain forgiveness of sin, live a useful life and look forward to heaven with Him.

REACHING OUT

Christ's last command requires us to reach out to our world with His gospel. We seek to help fulfil that by publishing books that point people towards Jesus and help them develop a Christ-like maturity. We aim to equip all levels of readers for life, work, ministry and mission.

Books in our adult range are published in three imprints.

Christian Focus contains popular works including biographies, commentaries, basic doctrine, and Christian living. Our children's books are also published in this imprint.

Mentor focuses on books written at a level suitable for Bible College and seminary students, pastors, and other serious readers; the imprint includes commentaries, doctrinal studies, examination of current issues, and church history.

Christian Heritage contains classic writings from the past.

For details of our titles visit us on our website
www.christianfocus.com

Christian Focus Publications Ltd
Geanies House, Fearn, Tain,
Ross-shire, IV20 ITW, Scotland, United Kingdom
info@christianfocus.com